ENRICH YOUR LIFE

twelve Bible studies on giving

Yvonne Vinkemulder

Inter-Varsity Christian Fellowship is a student movement
active on campus at hundreds of universities, colleges and
schools of nursing. For information about local and regional
activities, write IVCF, 233 Langdon St., Madison, WI 53703.

ISBN 0-87784-143-8

Printed in the United States of America

16	15	14	13	12	11	10	9	8	7	6
91	90	89	88	87	86	85	84	83	82	

"Enrich your life through Credit Bureau," proclaims a sign on a Madison bus. It reflects the value system of a society which says the good life consists of abundance of possessions. This emphasis is consistent with the very nature and make-up of people.

In contrast stands Paul's statement in 2 Corinthians 9: "You will be enriched in every way by great generosity." In other words, the good life consists not in acquiring but in giving.

And this is not the teaching of an isolated passage, but a thread woven throughout the Scripture: It is found in the books of the law, the historical narratives, the Bible's

4

poetry, the books of the prophets, the teachings of Jesus, and Paul's letters to young churches.

These twelve studies will take you into these writings from many different centuries and cultural settings, and help you find from Scripture itself a foundation for a right Christian perspective on giving—a subject often misunderstood or ignored. Spend twenty to thirty minutes a day with these passages. Write your findings in a notebook. Pray and act on the basis of what you learn. God will enrich your life!

Exodus 25:1-9; 35:5, 21-29; 36:2-7

1. Note the four aspects of the Lord's command in Exodus 25:1-9: (a) Moses' responsibility, (b) the character of those who give, (c) the nature of the offering, and (d) the function of the offering.

2. You may wish to skim through Exodus 1–19 for background. Note particularly the identity of the people of Israel in Egypt as slaves: afflicted, oppressed, broken in spirit, suffering under cruel bondage (1:11, 12; 2:23; 6:9). After a series of plagues or judgments meted out on the oppressor, the people were forcibly evicted from Egypt

(Ex. 12:29-39) and traveled through a wilderness unable to support two million or more people (12:37; 13:18; 15:22; 16:1, etc.). Consider their mode of travel, luggage restrictions, prospects of acquiring replacement goods. What was probably the source of any valuable goods they had (Ex. 3:21-22; 11:2-3; 12:35-36)? Given such a situation do you think you would be possessive or generous? Why?

3. Characterize those who responded to the Lord's command through Moses (Ex. 35:5, 21-29).

4. What was the measure and outcome of the people's response (Ex. 36:2-7)? Can you think of a particular ministry today which has this same "problem"?

2/THE EMERGING SOCIETY

Deuteronomy 14:22-29; 15:7-11; 16

1. Describe the tithe as to substance, frequency, place of "payment."

2. To what uses was it put (14:23, 26-27)? Why are the Levites singled out? (See Num. 18:6-7, 20-21 for background.)

3. What reason is given for the tithe (14:23)? Notice what they were tithing. How would this cause them to "learn to fear the Lord"? Describe their emotions as they obeyed.

4. Who else benefited from the annual tithe? What needs did the third-year tithe meet (cf. also Deut. 26:12-13)?

5. What was the responsibility of an Israelite to the poor (15:7-11)?

6. What is the significance of 15:9 (cf. vv. 1-5)?

7. Read 15:10-11. Notice the link between "cause and effect"—motive and result. What motivates your generous impulses? Do you think there are times when the need (v. 11) is there but blessing (v. 10) does not follow generosity? If so, what is your responsibility in such a case?

8. How often were adult males to appear before the Lord (16:16)? What one thing was required of them each time? Consider the significance of this in terms of time (16:3, 10, 13), inconvenience, wealth and material values.

9. What was required of them at the Feast of Weeks? Who was involved? Why was it appropriate that they should rejoice?

10. Compare the Feast of Booths in terms of time and attitude.

11. What does your giving contribute to others? to yourself? to God?

3/WORSHIP AND COMMITMENT

Deuteronomy 26

1. State the requirements given in verses 1-3. What declaration were they to make when offering the first fruits? How would this declaration and response set their frame of mind?

2. Why would this be an act of worship (v. 10)?

3. Compare this to a point (past or future) in your own life. If still looking ahead to such a point, what might you do as an act of meaningful worship?

4. Moses refers in 26:16-19 to statutes and ordinances beginning with 12:1 (and encompassing those cited in these two studies). How seriously were these to be taken?

5. By keeping the commandments of the Lord, what were the people declaring? What did God declare?

6. These statutes and ordinances were given with an agrarian society in mind. Translate the principles you've learned to an industrial or technical and largely urban society. If God's people today honored these principles, what effect do you think it would have on them? on those who minister to them spiritually? on the indigent and helpless (e.g., widows and orphans)?

7. What have you personally learned from this study to influence your values? What one practical change can you make in your daily life/habits that will reflect this lesson?

4/THE AFFLUENT SOCIETY

1 Chronicles 29

1. Review the context in chapter 28—especially verses 1-10. Why doesn't David go ahead with his dream? What injunction does he lay on Solomon?

2. Compare David's attitude and action

with his appeal to the assembly (vv. 3-5).

3. List the characteristics of God that David recognizes in this chapter. Compare David's description of himself and his people. Do you agree with his evaluation? Why or why not?

4. What is the ultimate source of the offering? How would your view of material things have caused you to respond?

5. Describe the spiritual condition and response of those who gave (vv. 9, 17-18). What do you think it means to offer with a "whole heart"?

6. What does David ask God to do for the people? for their new leader, Solomon? What might you have expected him to ask for?

7. To what climax does the liberal offering lead?

8. We no longer make animal sacrifices. Can you think of a parallel group experience we could have today which would result in gladness and the joyous praising of the Lord?

9. What connection do you see between

generosity and subsequent sacrifice and worship?

5/HERE COMES THE JUDGE
Psalms 37 and 50

1. State and summarize positive and negative commands in 37:1-8. What is the basis or source of confidence which justifies such an attitude?

2. In two columns contrast what the psalmist says about the wicked and about the righteous (vv. 12-33). Distinguish those statements that refer to *characteristics* of the righteous from those which refer to God's care for them.

3. If another person were to mark your character or relationship to God by these lists, would he classify you with the wicked or the righteous? In what ways can you cultivate generosity, wisdom and justice?

4. Summarize the expectations for the wicked and righteous (vv. 34-40). What accounts for the difference?

5. Distinguish between your attitude concerning injustice and your responsibility

in the face of it. What can you do today—this week—to reflect a righteous character?

Psalm 50

6. State the attributes or characteristics of God seen in 50:1-6 in relation to his office as judge. How extensive is his "court" (v. 1)?

7. What is his testimony concerning his people (vv. 7-15)? What are his commands?

8. What is his testimony against the wicked (vv. 16-22)? Contrast this to what he really desires (vv. 14-15).

9. How does thanksgiving honor God?

10. Does this song invalidate or enhance the sacrificial order given in the law? How?

11. What would the Mighty One testify concerning your sacrifices and offerings? Do you give to the Lord because you sense he needs it? out of gratitude and thanksgiving? for another reason?

12. Compare and contrast these two psalms in their descriptions of the righteous and the wicked. What have you learned to help you in God-pleasing living?

6/LET JUSTICE ROLL

Amos 5

1. Read the chapter several times, imagining that Israel is here facing her judge in a court of law.

2. Describe in your own words the outlook for Israel. Why is God's judgment so severe?

3. What is the solution (vv. 4, 6, 14-15)? Why is this the solution?

4. What one aspect of God's character is described in verses 8 and 9? What other aspect is alluded to in verse 15? From this chapter, what factors are involved in God's showing judgment or graciousness?

5. What relationship is there between God's accepting offerings and sacrifices and the actions of his people?

6. Contrast verses 7 and 24. What does God desire? How is this related specifically to the poor (v. 11)?

7. What relationship is there between your profession of social concern as a Christian and your action in terms of righteousness and justice? Consider this specifically in

terms of the pressing social needs of our cities and countries. Would God, in judging your giving and your service, be gracious or severe? For additional perspective, read and study Isaiah 58—59 and Micah 6.

7/SECOND BEST AND LEFTOVERS
Malachi 1:6-14; 3:6-12

1. Determine who is speaking, who is being addressed. Mark at least four descriptive terms claimed by the one speaking.

2. What is the point of interrogation in 1:6-10? What further declaration of attitude is revealed (v. 13)? Why does he suggest the radical remedy of 1:10?

3. Contrast the people addressed with those described in 1:11.

4. Contrast the character of the Lord with that of the sons of Jacob in 3:6-7.

5. Note again the use of interrogation in 3:7-8. What complaint does God register?

6. State the two commands and promises (3:7, 10-12). How are they related?

7. State the *two* sins described in these chapters. What is the specific responsibility

of the religious leaders? (Refer to Deut. 12, Mal. 2:4-9 if necessary.)

8. What is the relationship between attitude toward God and nature of the offering?

9. To what degree have you been giving the Lord of Hosts your second best or leftovers? What commitments can you make today to correct this sin?

8/FIRST THE KINGDOM
Matthew 6:19-34

1. Verses 22-24: "The eye here stands for interests, desires, ambitions, the directions in which attention is attracted . . . the whole character of man's life. . . . Mammon is an Aramaic word meaning 'wealth' and here stands for money and worldly interests" (*New Bible Commentary*). With these definitions in mind, compare the elements in the triplets of verses 19-24.

2. State the converse of verse 21. Would you agree to it? Why or why not?

3. What attitude is Jesus warning against? Why is this sin?

4. What is the relationship between

verses 19-24 and 25-34?

5. Contrast the goals of the Gentiles with those Jesus is teaching. With what kind are you preoccupied?

6. To what does "all these things" refer? In what ways are you pursuing or seeking the Kingdom of God and his righteousness? the things or gifts he gives?

7. Thank God for physical and material things he has given you. Ask him now to help you keep the right perspective . . . be specific!

9/COMMUNITY

Acts 4:32—5:11

1. List five or six characteristics of the believers in the early church.

2. Compare their attitude to the teaching of Jesus in Matthew 6. How does their "testimony to the resurrection" fit in?

3. Who was responsible for the distribution? Who were the recipients?

4. From Peter's statement, what options were open to Ananias and Sapphira? What was their sin? Write a few sentences as if you

were Ananias, explaining your action.

5. Compare the actions of Barnabas and Ananias. What happened to Ananias? to Barnabas (see Acts 9:27, 11:22-26, 13:1-3)?

6. Imagine yourself one of the believers. Consider the effect of God's judgment on you and the young church.

7. Note three descriptive phrases in the passage: "great power," "great grace," "great fear." What cause-and-effect relationships do you see between these and attitude toward possessions, testimony to the resurrection, growth of the church (vv. 12-14)? Which of these are characteristics of your life? Which should you ask God for?

8. Note again the phrase "those who believed were of one heart and soul." Does this characterize your relationship to other believers? How does it affect your use of God-given things—"yours" and "theirs"?

10/ADDED DIMENSION—GRACE
2 Corinthians 8

1. List six or seven characteristics of the churches of Macedonia.

2. Characterize the church at Corinth (v. 7). What additional quality does Paul want them to *excel* in?

3. State the three basic thoughts in verses 8-15. What is the relationship of equality to the tests of love and the will? To what extent is self-denial important? What evidence is there that *total* self-denial (i.e., to the extent that you deny your very personhood) is not implied? (If you disagree, state why.)

4. List all the facts you can find about Titus and the other brother mentioned in this chapter. What seems to be their specific role here?

5. What is the character and responsibility of the administrators of the liberal gift?

6. List all the references to "grace" and its derivatives. Relate "gracious work" to these other references. Why do you think Paul emphasizes this?

7. Meditate on verse 9. In what specific ways have you become rich because the Lord Jesus Christ became poor? To what action should his example lead you?

11/HARVEST OF RIGHTEOUSNESS

2 Corinthians 9

1. Compare the church at Corinth with those in Macedonia. Why is Paul sending the brethren?

2. Compare generosity to farming (vv. 6-10).

3. List the characteristics of generosity, stated in these two chapters, characteristics which you also found in your Old Testament studies.

4. Read the context of verse 9 in Psalm 112. What is the relationship between righteousness and generosity?

5. State at least six *effects* of generosity found in verses 6-15.

6. What is the *motive* for generosity (v. 13)? Why is obedience at this point a means of acknowledging the gospel? To what extent are you acknowledging the gospel through generous living?

7. What is the *dynamic* behind this kind of generosity? (Cf. 9:14 with 8:1, 7, 9.) Can you think of any reason why this is so? Who should get the credit if your generosity is

noticed and praised? How can you ensure this?

8. What is the supreme *example*? (Cf. 9:15 with 8:9.)

9. Analyze your motives for giving: habit? pressure? duty? desiring the result or effects (e.g., blessing/righteousness)? compelling desire? obedience? others? Ask God to help you examine your patterns of giving and determine, *by his grace,* to acknowledge the gospel by your obedience in this. You might ask him to bring to your attention one or more individuals or ministries which you can begin *now* to help.

12/A PRODUCTIVE PARTNERSHIP
Philippians 4:10-20

1. For what specific reason was Paul able to rejoice? How had the Philippians expressed their concern in the past? What does this imply about their present action?

2. In verses 11 and 12, compare Paul's varied circumstances and his attitude toward them. Which changes?

3. At this point, Paul was in prison for

the sake of the gospel—probably in Rome, perhaps in facilities rented at his own expense. What light does this shed on verses 10-13?

4. Look back at 1:3-8 and 4:1. How does Paul describe his relationship with the Philippians? What do you think each contributed to the relationship?

5. What two things does the gift from the Philippians accomplish? Which result does Paul really desire?

6. Have you entered into "partnership" with anyone in this way? What are the benefits to your partner? to you?

7. Who will care for the Philippians' needs? Who cares for yours? What connection is there between your generosity and the Lord's supply?

8. As you give (or receive) why should God receive glory? Does he? Ask God to show you how you can best contribute to his work, in ways that will (a) bring him glory, (b) benefit his workers, (c) enrich your own life.

InterVarsity Press is the book publishing division of Inter-Varsity Christian Fellowship. IVCF is a living, witnessing, praying, studying and singing fellowship of students and faculty at hundreds of U.S. universities, colleges and schools of nursing. It is one link in a chain of student work that encircles the globe through the International Fellowship of Evangelical Students. For information write Inter-Varsity Christian Fellowship, 233 Langdon, Madison, Wisconsin 53703 or phone 608-257-0263.